The Power of ONE Business Connection

How to Work by Referral
(book 1 of Five Part series)

Greg Petri

ISBN 978-1502794314

.

Table of Contents

(Note: Unattributed quotes are those of the author.)

“Networking is creating friendships that create opportunities in business and in life”— Greg Petri

Introduction

The main objective of this book is to inspire people to thrive and achieve more. ***"When your business becomes a conduit (an expression) for your life's purpose, you will thrive."*** This is a quote I made up, though inspired by Michael E. Gerber, author of one of the greatest books written about small businesses, *The E Myth;* he too sold encyclopedias for many years in California. I did this for 14 years to be exact.

It was one of those long ago times, before the Internet, before Google, when I learned how to do direct selling. It was an incredible learning experience. What the training taught me, by Macmillan Publishing, specifically Collier's Encyclopedias, was how to communicate with oil workers in Bakersfield, California, to executives working in Silicon Valley.

After realizing I needed to start my own company, One Business Connection was formed in July of 1997. The entire concept became clearer and clearer, that working by referral is one of the best ways to build a company, to get new clients and to thrive, and it is much, much easier than knocking on doors.

So after all these years, meeting thousands of business owners, entrepreneurs and sales professionals in almost every field you can imagine, this book has been drawn from their ideas and my interactions with so many amazing people.

Networking, working by referral, is a subset of marketing. And after meeting so many business professionals, it is also clear that the businesses that truly thrive have a commitment to finding better and better ways to market their companies.

How to work by referral is one of the most fun and easiest ways to grow your client base. I hope these ideas help you excel and thrive at whatever you have the desire to achieve so you too can fulfill your life's work, passion and purpose.

Greg Petri/Founder of One Business Connection, Inc

Contact Me Personally: 303.818.2460 or greg@onebusiness.com

Who Should Read This?

"One habit of the extremely wealthy is that they read at least 30 minutes a day on success and achievement." **— According to Success Magazine**

So you should read this and anyone who wants to improve their effectiveness in human communication, in the art and science of getting better at selling, networking, business, customer service, but more importantly, how to live an exceptional life.

How Should You Read This Book?

Read this book with an open mind. I guarantee – after being in my own business since 1997, and in networking and sales since 1980 – there will be many new ideas here. I also guarantee there will be ideas about which you say, "I know that; how obvious."

And this is what I ask: "Is it really that obvious? Or can you open your mind to an expanded piece of information that you may not be seeing?"

For example, Les Brown, one of the most powerful, exceptional and moving speakers of all times, used an obvious idea and expanded it to help people get out of what they know into what they don't know. Here is his insightful quote. Use this concept when reading this book: **"You don't know what you don't know … but you think you do."** A woman named Veronica Love called this cognitive blindness.

Try this one: "What you know is holding you back from knowing what you don't know."

Is what you are so certain of preventing you from getting and expanding into what you do not know? We all are guilty of this. For example, I occasionally get gout. It is generally known to be caused by eating certain kinds of foods. I believed I knew pretty much everything I needed to know about how to prevent it.

Then awhile back, I got a really bad gout attack. My big toe got so inflamed with uric acid deposits that I couldn't even sleep, hardly walk, barely work. So guess what? I decided maybe I really didn't know so much and I began doing research.

I found lots of new ideas, foods to eat, ways to prevent this ailment. It put me into a frame of mind that Tony Robbins talks about: CANI, Continuous and Never Ending Improvement. Huge pain and difficulty made me open my mind, discover new concepts and search for things that helped me know more about what I didn't know. And as Napoleon Hill said, "Every adversity has within it the seed of an equal or greater benefit." Look for your diamond in the rough, that jewel in all that you do, to expand what you know. Sometimes it's worth realizing that, "Adversity is the bridge to success."

I once had a friend who was so arrogant, so certain of what he knew, he wouldn't listen to anyone. I would joke with him, and tell him he would "argue with a dead man."

Don't be like that. Find the new ideas that can help you grow. Be aware. Pay attention. If you do this, you will get much from this book.

I wrote this book in small, digestible essays. Another way to read it is in daily ideas. Take just one idea (it may take you a couple of minutes to read), then put that idea into action for one day. Watch and see how that one concept, lived for a day, can make a huge difference in your business.

In all fields of knowledge, there are nuances, degrees, expanding points of view, breakthroughs that are just being discovered. Read this book with this in mind and you can glean the gems.

And an absolute fact: “Grow who you are and what you know, and you will grow your world, your opportunities and your enjoyment of life.”

What is Networking Anyway?

"The shortest distance between two sales is a well-handled and qualified referral."

In the standard definition, networking is a subset of marketing that gets the word out about your business and helps you get new clients. In practice, networking is "you advertising you" with personality and human communication. It is a three-dimensional way to grow your company. I call it "participation marketing," because you need to do something. It isn't a one-dimensional print ad that a person calls, not knowing who or what they will get.

In networking, the prospect gets you, your energy, your enthusiasm and your passion. They connect your business with a face, a real person, someone they know, a friend. This is what makes networking so magical, deeper than just dealing with a nameless, faceless corporation. Even if you work for a large corporation, a client still wants a connection with a face, a person they know, someone they can trust and depend on.

Networking is for everyone. Networking is becoming skillful at who you are, not just what you do. It is where you develop the skills of listening and figuring out how to be compelling when you do speak. Then people respect you and enjoy being around you.

And remember, you don't know what you don't know. Sometimes I look at networking like raising children: Everyone can do it. Most everyone does it – but do they really have a clue what they are doing? Are they exceptional at it, or are they doing it by default?

With this in mind, I recommend you adopt a few basic philosophies in your approach to networking to get the best results. In fact, creating better philosophies creates better results in all that you do.

Be Future-Oriented

Talk about it, plan for it, think about what you want and how to get it. Many define success as two simple things: Decide what you want and then get busy paying the price to make it happen. Optimistic people tend to have a future orientation. They talk about what they want, their vision, and they are excited about the opportunities and possibilities.

People who focus on the past generally are pessimistic people who complain about what happened before, how hard and difficult life is and has been. They talk about what they don't want, and by focusing on this, they create more of it.

In networking, being in control of a positive mental attitude is your choice. It really is the only thing you can control. Be positive, future-oriented and get the results you desire. "You can never get enough of what you don't want." — Russell Bishop.

So be optimistic. In networking, what are you selling? You are selling yourself. What are people buying? They are buying you. As Jeffrey Gitomer said, in his famous book, *The Sales Bible,* "People buy from friends." They are attracted to you because you have enthusiasm — you love what you do.

Have fun creating the vision and the life you want, and others will help you along the way because of your energy, your commitment to personal excellence. This is the absolute most important first step to becoming phenomenal in networking. And absolutely create a database from these connections you make. This may be the most valuable part of your business – compounding your database each week, month and year.

Be Genuine

If you are sincerely interested and fully attentive to what others say, what they are really communicating, their body language, their facial expressions, what they really want – guess what? They'll be interested in what you want, who you are, and in your dreams.

People see right through anyone who has the ability to influence others with their oratory excellence but, down deep, don't care about others. Be genuine: People will like you. You will like you.

Be kind

"Kindness is my true religion." — The 14th Dalai Lama

Really, what else is there in this life? Be nice, polite, friendly and willing to help others. Encourage everyone you meet. Find creative ways to keep in touch. Treat people like friends. Erase the dollar signs in your eyes, and see the person standing before you as a person, not as an object, but as someone you can help.

This doesn't mean you never have an upset moment, feel stressed or let life's issues get you down a little. But the more you want to help, care and be there for people, the more your brilliance will shine through. Then these connections you are making will amaze you, these people will begin to connect you to unbelievable opportunities.

Plant an apple tree and be willing to let it grow, no matter how long it takes before you get to pick off a ripe apple. Networking is more than just building relationships, it is "creating advocates." If I am an "advocate for you," and "you are an advocate for me," we can accomplish amazing things together. As you help others, sincerely, they also will want to help you and this long-term trust is what creates more and more opportunities, and more referrals in your business, too.

Who Really Should Network?

First, you do not "have to" network, you "get to" network. If you think of it as something exciting, as getting to know a lot of new and intriguing people, then you will enjoy it, rather than believe it is difficult.

I think there are many points of view here. You might even think, “I do not like to network.” And why is that? Maybe you think that it is hard, or manipulative, or that it just doesn’t apply to you because you run an automotive repair shop.

I say, if you have customers, you should want to network. If you want to create good energy with those loyal clients, you should want to network, and get good at creating a sense of trust and caring with the people you interact with.

Since networking is developing your communications skills, (the art of exceptional human interaction), it will help you in all your personal interactions, in business, in family, in any relationship. And your meaningful relationships are what make life so rewarding and rich. Be good in this area of your life, and you will succeed at most everything you do.

First Step to Networking

"Success is clarity." — Brian Tracy

Get clear not only about what you want, but also what you love to do. Get clear on what your big dreams are, the ones that stir your soul, and then commit to making these things happen. Clarity and definiteness of purpose elevate you beyond the ordinary into the extraordinary. It's this clarification that puts tons of coal into the engine that fuels your passion, to get you from where you are now to the vision you see in your mind's eye of where you want to arrive. A person with true and clear purpose will attract the right people and opportunities that others can't even see or imagine.

How to do this? The first step is to find out your bottom line, your "why." Why do you want to accomplish your highest aspirations?

Once you are clear about your commitment, then clarify your values. Sometimes the idea "what are my values" confuses people, as it seems a nebulous, hard-to-access, indefinable set of vague internal rules.

Values are the intangibles that all the tangibles are built upon — ideals only you can identify, such as integrity, peace, love, compassion, passion, truth, honesty, action and creativity, to name a few.

One of the easiest ways to discover your values is to ask yourself: What is valuable to me? Determination and persistence are valuable to me. Doing what I say I will do is valuable to me.

If you're still not sure, notice the traits you admire in others, and you will begin to discover, uncover and clearly understand what makes you tick. Values motivate you toward your goals and also give you a reference point to ensure you stay true to who you are on the road to your dreams.

Once you've identified your own values, burn them into your conscious mind, so you know 100% what makes you take action. Again, this clarity in being attracts the right people to you. This is the first, maybe the most important step to becoming incredible at networking.

One value may encompass three or four similar subvalues, so take your time. Identify not only what a value means, but also what it means to you. For example, integrity: This is usually one of everyone's top values. Everyone *says* they have integrity. Now, how can this be?

Define with total clarity what integrity means to you and commit that definition to your mind so you will live by it most of the time. And it is not hard to understand that integrity, depending on your understanding and definition, can include honesty, peace and even persistence.

Values such as integrity may be fussy around the edges. You may have a lot of integrity in one area of your life but lack it when faced with a boss or an authority figure where you do what is expected rather than being true to yourself. Continually create better definitions and understandings of your most sacred values.

Values are not static. They will change. You can redefine and refine your values in the months or years ahead. So take time. Do not rush. Make your values, goals, dreams and worthy ideals clear, and you not only will be successful in networking, but also will accomplish what you want in life. People love to be around others who are focused and clear about what they want and are confident with who they are. This attracts the right mindset and right people to you, and that is what networking is all about. Think of it as less technique and *more about who you are*.

There are many values, but I think it is better to have or be clear about three values (up to, but no more than four or five if they are extremely meaningful to you) and commit to them. This will form the rock-solid foundation to build your dreams upon.

Start here. This will give you the energy, the passion, the enthusiasm that will fuel all your networking efforts.

According to motivational speaker Chris Widener, "People are either moving toward or away from you." The reason for this is your passion, your commitment to excellence, your level of excitement and your passionate way of living. Everyone wants a piece of the visionary, the excited and charismatic individual. You will be charismatic proportional to the clarification of your values, and your commitment to take action (to completion) toward your dreams. Your goals make up the vision that is behind it all.

Get clear on what you want. Put in the effort it will take to get to that clarification of understanding your values.

Make it important today to clarify your values, to set up your goals on paper. Write them down. Read them every day. Create daily action steps. It has been said if you want to be in the top 3% of all people on planet Earth, write down your goals. Jim Rohn also said, "Only 3% of all people have a library card." Is there a connection perhaps?

To Earn More, You Have to Learn More

To be in the top 1% of all people, write down your goals daily. How long does this really take, two or three minutes a day to be in the top 1%? Then to be in the top .5%, put a simple action step under each goal, and make a daily appointment to confirm that you are doing these daily action steps.

Once a week, write down each goal and put a "why" underneath it. Why do I really want to accomplish this? This puts you beyond almost everyone in creating the life you want. This will attract other brilliant people to you. In the words of

Zig Ziglar, “You move from being a wandering generality into becoming a meaningful specific.”

Also, write down grateful goals, what you have right now that you can appreciate. This helps us all to enjoy what is really valuable. Do you have children? What can be more important than playing or spending time with them or your loved ones?

3 Secrets to Successful Networking

Secret #1

Be likable. Be friendly. Be polite. Be kind. Go out of your way to help and serve. Do more than people expect. Genuinely care about other people. When you do this with sincerity and with heart, then you will be on your way to being a powerful networking expert.

Don't let people who are going nowhere, who have little or no motivation or sense of urgency, take up a lot of your time. This is a very fine line to walk and a tactful balancing act to perfect. And the only way to be likable is to like yourself, to be excited about your life, who you are and where you are going.

Have a purpose, an enlightened attitude about the meaning of life, your life. Be peaceful with who you are. Then you are likable. Also, work on yourself, your tact, your delivery, the way you say things, the way you show up. "Not only be present but have a presence." We can all get better at who we are, or at least acknowledge our true power. Find better ways to encourage, to listen, to care, to serve. This will attract like-minded people, individuals who help you and you can help.

Secret #2

Improve your communication. How you communicate with others is vital. Are you articulate? Are you interesting? Do you listen actively and take an interest in others? Do you stand tall, lean forward and listen intently when someone is talking to you? Do you give them your absolute, complete and undivided attention? Do you have good eye contact? Do your eyes move all over the place, when they should be intently focusing on who you are speaking with right now? Do you treat everyone as if they are a million-dollar client?

One of the biggest issues in networking is that everything has gone so far online – with virtual this, online that – that many people (especially younger ones) need more help than ever in how to effectively communicate face to face. There are skills that can be learned and must be learned to be effective with new people, co-workers, family and even children. Continually improve your skill sets here to become a charismatic and compelling speaker, and an intent listener.

Be a leader: This world needs more leaders, especially young, entrepreneurial ones.

Body language is essential. What matters here is your intonation, voice fluctuation, enunciation, tonality, your smile, your posture, how you stand, how you move, your higher states of awareness. Concentrate on being interesting (and interested in others) with your body language and your energy.

It is so easy to become habitual, ordinary and not aware of your posture, your pauses in speech or your voice inflections. It is so easy to say, "Hey, I know how to network, I have done it over and over so many times. What's the big deal?" The big deal is that you want to get massive results and get out of habitual mediocrity.

Use your body language to get attention, intrigue and to pique interest. Get better at how you show up, how you dress and your presence of being, and you will improve your communication skills. People will take notice. Again, we can get more skillful at this.

Take time to improve, to learn more, to motivate and to inspire people, to inspire yourself.

According to NLP (Neuro Linguistic Programming), communication is 7% the words you use, 38% intonations, 55% body language. Master all forms of human communication. Show up in a Peak State of Performance.

Secret #3

Invest time with others, not just a half-hour meeting, but time spent over months, sometimes years, to create these advocates. In networking, you want to make long-term affiliations, create relationships, but more importantly (this is worth repeating): Create advocates. If I am an advocate for you, and you are an advocate for me, we will find incredible ways to refer and help each other.

Create relationships that last. First, get to know who a person is. This is so much more important than what they do. What are their dreams, their interests, what is important to them? Dig in. Really get to know who people are and you will create more than business connections – you will create new friendships.

Friends help each other, buy from each other and refer business to each other. A connection based on trust and respect will last. As Warren Buffet once said, "Don't do business with people who churn your stomach." Surround yourself with excited and motivated people. Be very careful about letting certain people drag you down — you know who these people are.

Even in my personal life, I have noticed that my young daughter is so much more caring and loving to me, she loves her daddy, not when I buy her more stuff, or give her more sugar, but when I play with her, spend time with her, be with her. What else is there, really?

Why Have a Commitment to Networking?

"Success is a decision." – But You Knew That, Right?

The more you network, the more you will learn what's new and innovative in the marketplace. Things change so fast and networking puts you in front of innovators, people on the cutting edge of new technologies, new ideas and ways of marketing and doing better business.

Networking is the curious way to discover the new things other people know and do. Everyone you meet is an open book. Learn from them.

Networking gives you an advantage. Expand what you know, and that knowledge makes you more valuable to your clients. The more you know, the more you can help others and the bigger impact you can have on your own career and this world. This makes life interesting. "Life is an adventure; dare it." – Mother Teresa.

Network not because you are "supposed to," but because of the added-value benefits. The extra perks are that you get to be better informed and live a stimulating life. You will meet people who do so many crazy and intriguing things. Not long ago, at a networking event, I met a man who created a $500 million company in one year. Pretty amazing.

Networking is what people do and the more you do it, the more skills you will perfect. Network to grow who you are and grow what you think you know. Also, network for other people: The connections may be valuable to you, but can be even more valuable to the trusted clients and people you already know. Network for yourself and all the other people you know in your network.

Once, I went to an Italian business networking event. I met a tax lawyer. I immediately thought he would be a great connection for some of the CPAs I know and some of the other lawyers who do different kinds of law.

Fifty percent of all people who reach the age of 85 get Alzheimer's disease. One proven way to prevent this insidious disease is to continually learn, read, discover. You have heard it a million times that you need to learn more. But how often do you shut off the TV to read a book? How often do you take a new way home?

Challenge yourself. Become an expert at what you do by studying, researching and becoming the absolute best you can be, then do even more than that. Commit to excellence. Fight against mediocrity. Again, have a commitment to what Tony Robbins calls Continuous and Never Ending Improvement.

Matt Morris, a young, multimillion-dollar entrepreneur, says, "Read five books in any area and you become an expert. You will know 95% more than anyone on the subject." Why not?

Networking is a way to expand who you know and what you know, and to learn about all the new ideas, products and services that weren't even around a few months ago. Networking is one of the ways, your way, to keep pace with burgeoning changes in the world of business, finance, health, technology and many other fields of knowledge.

As you learn more, people will respect your opinions, and ask for your advice and ideas, and you also will become a "go-to person" when they need someone or something. Your expanding connections are how you become more and more valuable to everyone you know.

One of the easiest ways to attract the right people, circumstances and opportunities to yourself is to be aware, and in a continual and awe-inspiring state of mind, which will create more options in your life. This will keep you in new mind, "beginner's mind," so you not only see, enjoy and investigate new opportunities, but you also act on them, incorporate and assimilate them into your expanding arsenal of knowledge that settles into a practical, common-sense wisdom that you can use in life, business and all your relationships. This adds value to all that you do.

Forever be curious and in awe. "Curiosity never killed anything." Look to what is innovative. See the unfolding opportunities everywhere. Believe you live on the absolute cutting edge of evolution, and it is not only an amazing time to be alive, but the only time that offers such changing and accelerated information and knowledge that can add to your expanding view of business and life.

Today, set appointments to meet new people who are doing things you know little about. Create daily, weekly, monthly and yearly goals – networking goals – and track and measure your results. Begin pushing yourself **"out there"** to get to know more new people. What if you said I will meet two new people a day, and added them to your database? This will help you discover new ideas and new paradigms of thinking. I know someone who makes 25 calls a day. After 20 years in business, he knows many people and is extremely successful.

Go to events and trade shows that are not part of your target market, just to expose yourself to other industries and new people. The more you network and get excited about the plethora of creative ideas, alternative products, services and profound people, then the more you expand what you know, what you can do, and how you can creatively and effectively conjugate and expand your world.

Network = Net worth

"Set income goals for your networking."

Who do you really care about? Trick question? I don't think so. You care about people who care about you. You care about a person who takes time to listen to you, who returns your calls, who is enthusiastic about life, about what they do, who continually talks about opportunities that are everywhere on this planet.

So if you value people who care, listen and take an active interest in your life, then it's simple to get results in networking. Be that person, too, and you will get the results you seek. "Networking is to travel through time with friends and people who you care about." A friend I met through networking called me on a summer afternoon just to tell me about a bumper sticker they saw: "Be more wag and less bark."

When you care, people know it. People can see through any manipulation, any skillful strategies and learned techniques. "Be yourself because everyone else is taken." — Oscar Wilde.

People to network with are those who take a moment to do these things out of genuineness, not because it is a good marketing idea. Find the people you like, who do not churn your stomach, who are just as interested in your success as they are their own. These "good-as-gold" people are the people to seek out, find and help.

Spending time with people who are kind and caring and willing to help you, too, will make your life and business easy instead of a struggle. Who in the world said you had to spend time with problem children and those who aggravate more than they give back?

You have heard this expression: High-maintenance people. They're not the ones to hang out with. Spend time with those who are positive and uplifting. This is the fastest track to success. "You don't have to eliminate everyone in your life who are negative, just limit your exposure."

"If you want to succeed faster, give your worst clients to your competitors."

Take time with the right people. Take an interest in their successes and misadventures, their ways of running or backing across the finish line, and you will begin to reap the rewards, revel in the marvels, enjoy meeting new people and discovering different ways to help them. And you will find an army of people wanting to help you too.

Networking is one of the best ways to grow your company, to be in good company, to accompany those with a dream. Charles Gregory once said, "When you are in good company, you are in a good company."

Networking should be your lifeblood, the four pillars in place around the magnificent dream you are building. With this dedication to people, you will get the results through who you know. Then you can achieve anything. Networking is where you will find the most enjoyment out of your work, the most satisfaction in the ebb and flow of building a company as you create advocates, friendships and relationships that enhance the excitement of creating more success. ***"Never take lightly the power of the connections you are making."***

Where to Network

I once asked a very successful financial planner, how he made time to go skiing 35 times a year, and he said, *"I put it in my day planner."* — David M.

So you are going to, or you have committed someone in your organization, to go to networking events, to grow your company and your client base. However, there's a lot more to this than just showing up. You may be an expert at what you do. Now become an expert at networking. But please, don't use the excuse that you are too busy.

Before you network, figure out what a real networking event is, and where you can go to get the connections you want. In the United States, a traditional networking event is a monthly after-hours event at a local chamber. If you are a chamber member, be sure to check their website for breakfast meetings, luncheons, trade shows, as well as educational events — all great opportunities to meet lots of people.

Other places to network are Rotary Clubs, church socials and professional referral groups. Trade shows, industry-specific events such as home and garden shows, and seminars, are also perfect places to network between speakers and during breaks. Just make a commitment to meet new people, especially at seminars, where the main focus is sitting and listening.

Of course, one of the absolute best ways to find places to network is search the Internet for "where to network" in your area. You will find many options. Get good at meeting people. Every card you get is potentially a new client or a string of referrals coming to you soon.

Be creative. Going to a baseball game, a Boy Scout meeting, anywhere people get together can be an opportunity to ask people what they do and get some business cards. Have a goal to say meet two to three new people every day. You may want to set this goal even higher. This way it pushes you to engage, talk to people when you are in an elevator, sitting in a waiting room or standing in line at the grocery store, as you now have a goal to achieve.

Once you place yourself in situations to meet more people, the next level is to add skills that will help you make the most of the opportunities you have created.

How to Get Results at the Events You Attend: Set Goals!

Plan ahead. How many networking events will you attend in the next month? How many people do you plan to meet? How many connections or referrals are you going to generate? How much income will you generate from these connections? And, of course, do you have a plan or system to follow up with them and add them to an effective database?

Say you are going to an after-hours event at a chamber. Always set a goal for the number of people you want to meet at any event. Say there will be 200 people attending. Your goal might be to meet and make contact with 20 new people. Of course you know this, but you can’t hit a target you don‘t have.

Get a target number in your head. Having a goal will give you the impetus not only to meet new people but also to politely excuse yourself and keep reaching out to gather more business cards and meet other interesting people. To keep talking to people you already know is easy, but it defeats the purpose of effective networking.

Most people attend events to just mingle. Few if any, have an exact goal. For example, I once went to a chamber event. My goal was to meet 18 new people and get their business cards. I left the event, looked in my shirt pocket, counted the cards and there were exactly 18. Chance? I don't think so.

I looked at the cards, and there were two that were the same, a duplicate. Then I looked on the back of one and written there was contact information for a person because she didn't have any business cards with her. Again, exactly 18. Hitting an exact number has happened to me many times. It is an intention. Put an intention out there for almost anything: Income goals, people to meet, whatever, and if you "really believe it in your heart," then you will see that intention begin to happen.

In networking I have developed a **Success Tracker** that tracks income, events, contacts face-to-face meetings, which always works if you do. Set an intention, take action on that intention and it becomes real. "What gets measured gets results." Don't just see what happens, or hope something will come out of your going to events. Set a goal and watch the magic happen.

Be Interested

According to Chris Widener, motivational speaker and New York Times best-selling author, when you meet new people, strive to be "interested" more than "interesting." People like to talk about themselves, and usually think favorably about others who show genuine interest. When you get the inevitable question, "So, what do you do?" Open with a preplanned answer that intrigues the listener to ask for more information. And as Brian Tracy would say, as soon as possible, turn the spotlight back on them. To listen is huge, for it helps you find out what others need, who they are, what they are interested in.

Be so compelling with your attention and with your sincere interest that the person you are speaking with will remember you. This is the first step to building a relationship. You can be interested by asking better questions, open-ended questions that get people to explain: "What do you mean by that, or can you give me an example?"

The better you get at sincere questions, the more you can get almost anyone to talk about themselves. This opens up endless opportunities, if you are creative enough to realize there is always something they said, they do, they enjoy that can create common ground so as to begin a relationship that can help you and them, too.

Another idea, given the choice, it's better to get a business card than to give one out. Why? It puts you in control to follow up quickly. I never hand out a business card unless someone asks. If they ask, what does that mean, or tell you? I think it tells you that they are interested in you or nice enough or polite enough to want to know what you do. Either way, I usually follow up within 48 hours.

You can connect on social media, phone or email or even a text. There are now so many ways to follow up with people. The best is to find out what they prefer, put a little note on the back of a card, i.e., "They like email better than phone calls." You will connect up faster and easier if you know their preferred way of communication.

Be Professional

Dress nicely, smile, be polite and exude excellence. You are a professional. Act with an air of confidence, presence and resolve. Your first impression can affect and have tremendous influence on your second meeting. Be confident but not arrogant. Be light, humorous and be pleasant. No one gets too excited being around people who are too serious.

Be a Connector

Recently, I went to a chamber after-hours event. I met a person who did residential solar. Later, I met a rep for another company that did mostly commercial solar panels. I introduced them right there at the event. And even if you don't have a chance to introduce them at the event, when you call or contact them the next day to follow up, mention you just met someone who could be a good connection. Helping others, without thinking there is something in it for yourself, can (and usually does) create the most incredible opportunities in ways you cannot even see or realize right now.

This impresses people and shows you really care. Do this to help. Good things come from just helping without expecting anything in return. Sure, it is easy to think about, but can you really help without expecting anything at all in return? It is not that easy, but it gets results in the most unusual and magical ways.

And when you do create a long-term relationship, then people consider you a resource that brings people together. Always thinking about who you can connect up with who; this will pay dividends in goodwill alone. And goodwill is a quantifiable value in any business. Just ask the IRS or business brokers who do business valuations before a sale.

And again, when networking, keep in mind that you are not just networking for yourself, to get connections for yourself and for your company. You are networking to meet many new people who could be great connections for all the other people you know. For you are not just helping yourself in your networking efforts, but also can help many people with your efforts.

I once met a woman who owned a nonprofit and I introduced her to another nonprofit. They helped each other grow a nationwide company. Wow!

So remind yourself, when networking, always think if the person you are talking with can be a good connection for other people you know. Then when you come across someone that may not be the ideal connection for you, you still can find ways to help them, and introduce them to your loyal clients and people you know who may be ideal connections, power partners, resources and centers of influence.

Small Things to Remember in Networking

When in a networking meeting, referral group or a sit-down meeting, stand up and speak up. Project your voice. Bring props. I have had chiropractors come to my networking groups and bring plastic spines. Do something different. Stand on your chair. Walk around the room. Do things in memorable and creative ways. I have had people sing their personal introductions. Have fun; what else is there anyway?

When at any networking event, or a place to meet new people, make sure you wear your nametag on the right side of your chest. That is where people's eyes look first. Sometimes I will wear my nametag on my leg just to be different. To get noticed, and be remembered, is the objective. Find creative ways to make an impression. People like people who are light on their feet and who are unique. I was once in a resort area that sold souvenirs. I bought one that was engraved on wood. It said, "You are unique, just like everyone else." Ha.

Shine your shoes, iron your clothes, brush your teeth and smile. Get some "networking mints." Often, I have met people whose breath was so bad, I really felt like telling them. I guess that is one way to make a lasting impression. Maybe I should've said, "Here, would you like a mint?"

Stand up Straight

Continually scan and check your posture. It has been said a person slumped over with eyes looking at the ground thinks mostly of the past, and worries about their problems. This automatically repels the optimistic people. A person upright, standing tall, attracts the right people to themselves, those who are also powerful and successful people.

Even if you are on the phone, on a conference call, in a webinar, or in a place where you cannot even be seen, stand up, dress sharply and smile in the mirror, for this adds to and influences all of your verbal communications in a productive and effective way.

Be attentive. Pay attention. Look people in the eyes and listen intently to what they are saying. Listen with your entire body. Be aware. Be alert. Notice things others don't see. Be so conscious of others that it impresses them that you noticed their red brooch, the logo on their business card or whatever. There is always something to discover, to notice, to accentuate. Be a person of heightened awareness. People will notice and be impressed.

Take a Risk

Do something different. Be creative. Be a person willing to take a risk, to step over the line, yet be pleasant without ego. People love to be around someone who is willing to stick their neck out, so do something unusual. But be tactful, of course, and you will attract the kinds of people you want and need if you have enough self-awareness to sand off the rough edges of your personality.

"Risk is jumping off a cliff and building your wings on the way down." — Ray Bradbury

Be Personable

Be charming and a pleasure to be around. Never argue or be too opinionated with someone you just met. Let others be opinionated. According to Bob Berg, "You can even talk to anyone about religion and politics as long as you agree with them."

Let others be the star and shine. You be the conduit, the one who is interested — because if you try, you always will find most people intriguing. You can always uncover something that is different or unique about someone. Do this and you are remembered, and you also will remember them. By treating people like they are the most important person on Earth, your networking will get more results than all the flamboyancy and self-promotions you could ever come up with.

Take Time To Meet Them After You Meet Them

In networking, there is a concept: Take the time to build relationships. This means, take the time to meet one on one outside of normal networking events to get to know someone. Many people know this, but don't really understand the power of this until they do it consistently. Find out more about who people are, rather than just what they do. Meet with people, again and again, to find out what their dreams are, their passions, their ideas of what they want to do and become. Do this and you'll amplify the effectiveness of your networking exponentially.

Be inspiring. People don't often meet inspirational people. Do this and you will keep yourself inspired. And to create a better business, more contacts, more opportunities, find ways to inspire yourself — and this also will inspire others. And the best way to be inspired is to learn new things, and love what you are doing, moment by moment. "If you do what you love to do you will never work another day in your life." — Confucius. It may take time, but the by-product of meeting people outside or after you have met them at a networking event is that it almost always generates new referrals for them and you, and opportunities you never thought of.

In our networking organization, One Business Connection, I ask people to do these "member meetings." Some organizations call them dance cards, relationship builders, one on ones. Whatever the name, the reason for doing a lot of these meetings is not to sell products or services, but to create deeper relationships.

Do this consistently, and your network will grow massively. And isn't this true: No matter what your business, your goal is to grow your clients, and these clients are who keep you in business? You may be in network marketing; your goal is to build a team. You are an auto mechanic shop; your goal is to get new clients. Networking builds your client base. Brian Tracy has said, "The purpose of business is to get new clients and keep those clients."

Not only do this, but also track and measure. Do 10, 20 or more of these outside meetings each month. Set a goal. Track and measure, and you will see results you cannot even imagine. Just don't get jaded by thinking people are just wasting your time, not buying your products or services, or they are just not the right connection. Think long term, and with an open heart and mind. You will begin to see the possibilities others don't.

So when you meet someone at a networking event who seems interesting, invite them to lunch, or set up a meeting for a half-hour before the next networking event. You may also consider meeting for a happy hour, or even set up an outdoor or recreational activity such as golf, skiing or attending an athletic event together. One of the most exciting member meetings I ever had was flying in a glider 3,000 feet over Boulder, Colorado. It was pure excitement.

What you believe becomes your reality. Don't believe you are too busy. We are all busy. Was Bill Gates too busy to run a worldwide company? Saying that you are too busy is an excuse. The point is, take time with people, create alliances and build friendships, and these connections will bear fruit, creating new clients, new opportunities and resources. When you take the time to get to know people, you become more than a product or a service provider; you become a resource and a wealth of information, a person and a friend. ***"Who you know is many times more valuable to your clients (and the people you meet) than what you sell."***

For example, you meet a flooring person. The next day, a client of yours needs wood floors installed. You connect the two. Everyone wins. You win by being a resource beyond the product or services you provide. Your client wins because they get some really cool hardwood flooring at a great price. And your new flooring connection wins by getting more business. I will tell you this: Close a sale or help someone get a new client, and you create long term loyalty.

If you help others, what is their natural response? They now want to find a way to help you. This is called the law of reciprocity. Sometimes, simply trying to help is just as important as really helping. This is the heartbeat of networking, planting seeds and harvesting goodwill. Your giving and caring can do nothing but come back to you like a boomerang.

Set aside time before or after the next networking event and get to know someone you have just met. You will find common ground and ways to help them.

What is this life about anyway, but to meet people, share with others, find ways to help one another and enjoy the process? I once read a quote: “Love all, serve all.” There’s not much else.

Do this and you will discover the rewards are like stumbling into a gold mine picking up new connections that are more valuable than nuggets of gold.

Breaking the Ice

"Argue for your limitations and you shall keep them." — Richard Bach, Illusions

Plan out your events. Say, "Yes, I am going to more seminars. Yes, I am going to more chamber events, trade shows, places where my target market meets." Realize and believe you are a walking billboard for what you do, and that you are obligated by God to talk to anyone within a 10-foot radius about what you do. You might say, "I don't have time to do all that." And I say, you probably do, but if not, hire someone. Train an employee or sales rep on how to network and they will get a ton of new business for your company.

But really, once you get to an event, how do you go up to someone and begin speaking? How do you ***break the ice?*** Most people are shy and introverted, and even those who seem very outgoing will admit (behind closed doors) that they are a little reserved when in front of new people.

When you're nervous, the tendency might be to wait until someone talks to you and then start rambling on about yourself, not letting the other person get in a word. Ask better questions and you will get better responses.

I usually look for someone who is not talking to anyone, and just go over to them and say something like, "Can I meet you?" What are they going to say, "No sorry, I am here at this networking event to meet people, but not you"? Bob Berg says the most influential people to meet are the ones who have people around them, and people keep looking to the leader of that group for their responses.

Keep a mental note of these people, and then approach them later when not around a lot of others. I say anyone can be a great connection, everyone has a story to tell and will be a resource for you and you for them — unless they are extremely negative and pessimistic.

And when you do meet someone, ask open-ended questions that do not have a yes or no answer, for example: "How did you get into this field of work?" The more you get people talking, the more comfortable you become and guess what? The more they talk, very soon they probably will give you ideas about how you may help them. When you meet at a later date, more in depth, this information is invaluable.

Ask some well-thought-out questions, for this opens the door for you to get new ideas and information, and make friends, not just business associations. People know when you are being artificial, manipulative or insincere.

People love to talk about themselves. Let them. Encourage them. Make a comment about the event, or their red shoes, anything to make first contact in a pleasant and open way. Use humor and be in a good mood. People are attracted to nice, excited and inspired people. Plus, do it more often, go to more events. As you go to more events, practice and engage, you will get better and better at breaking the ice, establishing a rapport and being exceptional at meeting new people.

After you set a rapport, one of the best questions to ask, according to Bob Berg, who wrote a book called "Endless Referrals," is, "So when I am talking to someone, how would I know that they would be a good connection or client for you?"

People are at these business events to meet new people, so they want to talk to you. Realize this, and you will be able to talk to anyone. Talk from your heart; it takes much less technique, and just common sense, and being real with people. How easy is that? People are at a networking event because they want to explain what they do. They want to make new associations, so let them.

If someone is rude, cold or disinterested, or not in the right mood, just say, "It was nice meeting you. I'm going to talk to a few other people." In many ways it is a numbers game. The more people you talk to, sooner or later you will meet individuals you feel comfortable with, and these are the people to follow up with the next day. You know intuitively if someone is a great connection. Plus, if you have a goal before you get to the event, this motivates you to hit that target, goal or number of connections you would like to make.

Other Ways to Amplify Your Success

First, change the jargon, chatter and belief structures in your own head. Why are people at networking events? They come to expand their sphere of influence and to meet new people, most often to get new clients to help their company grow. When you approach new people with this certainty and common purpose, it is easy. Be there to help, give and serve, and you will find incredible ways to connect with people you do not yet know.

And as crazy as this sounds, you will run into people who have no business cards. Do not just give them one of yours, as you have no control on future contact. Always bring a pen so you can write down their name, phone number, even email or a personal note, on the back of another's business card or slip of paper so you can follow up with them. And of course, make sure you have business cards, a pen, and your cellphone, as these are just basics to have when going to any networking event.

And yes, believe whomever you are talking to is intriguing, and has ideas and new things they are doing that you are interested in and you want to know more about. Be truly interested. Don't just act interested. Then you will learn a lot, and your genuine nature will attract them to want to know more about you, too. If you deeply take an interest, you can find something of value in everyone you meet. Treat people as if they are the most important person you have talked to all night. This will compliment them, make them feel good about who they are and make you one of the most memorable people they met at the event.

So when they are talking to you, do not be distracted or looking around. Give them your full attention. Do this with new people. Do this with people you know. Do this with your children, the people you care about, and you will see a huge shift in their energy too.

This attracts people to you to get not only *better* results, but *incredible* results. You, by your sheer energy, by who you are, by being the best you can be, naturally will attract the right people to you. By continually working on who you are, removing limits in your own mind, enjoying life in each moment and enjoying the things you do, these are the best ways to break the ice with new people, expand your database, and turn new contacts into friends, clients and resources.

Make it a habit to introduce yourself to people. No matter where you go, even if it is not a scheduled and organized event — in elevators, in restaurants, at parties, at art shows, plays, standing in line for food. I once introduced myself to a waitress whose father was a business owner, and she gave me his phone number. I called him and he became a client.

Through the years, this connection directly and indirectly has generated thousands of dollars for my company. Set a goal of the number of new people you will meet not only at this event, but each day and each week. A goal gets results, otherwise whatever happens happens, and it is usually not what you want or expect. Anticipations, higher expectations and intentions get you the results you want. Do not network by default, as most people really do, just to see what happens. Be intentional in your networking efforts. This will get the results you desire.

"Again, there are no fences in your head." Your only limitations are self-imposed. Realize there is always a better, more effective way to do anything. So try new approaches. Watch what others do, and you will get better at breaking the ice, at meeting new people. But more than that, you will become better at who you are, and this attracts the right new people you need to grow your company.

And, when you are at a networking event, keep going, keep prospecting, and find polite and tactful ways to move on so you can meet the number of people you want to. If you meet a phenomenal connection, sure you can take more time. But what I see over and over at these events are people talking for long periods of time with the same person, or people they already know. When I know two people well and see them at a networking event, talking and talking to each other, I go over to them and say in a humorous way, "You are supposed to talk to people you don't know." And I smile and they smile, and they keep talking to the same person. Oh well, at least I tried to help.

The Greatest Skill

Every great dream will involve people, a lot of people, and you need people skills to amplify and multiply your success and accelerate your journey to your goals. Networking is becoming so tactful and skillful at human communication that you excel.

There are always new ideas, new ways to do this, so keep an open mind. For the art of communication is forever expanding, and it is probably the most valued skill in business and human relationships that you will ever develop.

Networking skills positively affect all aspects of your life. Think about this. Get better at networking, and you will improve all your personal relationships. You will be a better manager of employees, dealing with co-workers and employers. You will be able to relate to bosses, friends, family and associates much better. These remarkable communication and networking skills will create more energy, focus and effectiveness in all your interactions. You will discover how to give more, care more and create opportunities for others. People will like you. You will like you. You will develop and deepen your relationships with the people you care about the most. You will discover that you attract the "good-as-gold" and right people into your life right now.

Many people have blind spots in their abilities and skills to communicate. Usually they do not even see their tactlessness, or their shortness, rudeness or hurried and impolite behaviors. Learn more expanded and progressive skills, and you will excel and shine beyond most all people struggling for more effective communication.

As you meet all these interesting people doing so many interesting things, you will learn so many new things that you will become a generalist, an informed and knowledgeable person in many fields. You then can use this breadth of knowledge and common sense to help others to also be more informed.

As you become confident in your networking skills, you will begin to see the indomitable spirit in all you meet. You will begin to stretch, think bigger, become someone who says and believes, “Everything is possible, and opportunity is everywhere.” — Robert Kiyosaki.

Michael Jordan once said, "Obstacles don't have to stop you. If you run into a wall, don’t turn around and give up. Figure out how to climb it, go through it or work around it." Networking skills will teach you how to get through any wall, to dig under it, to hire a crane, to rent a bulldozer. This will teach you to do whatever it takes to get through that wall. Why?

Because in networking, you will meet extraordinary people who will inspire you to do more than you ever thought you could. You will encounter people with passion, so much passion, you will realize, failure is not an option, it's just a storm passing through. You will meet others who do what you have only dreamed about doing.

Becoming skillful at networking will refine your personality if you let it. You will get better at public speaking and listening, finding ways to understanding and caring about someone else's dream. You will develop tact, which is the cornerstone of all heightened communication. And I bet you have come across that rude person who has absolutely no tact, and defends their rudeness by saying, ''I am just being honest."

It is like the Pareto Principle: 80% of the people you meet when networking will not be very good at it. The other 20% may amaze you. Learn from them.

As Charlie "Tremendous" Jones once said, "If you hang around with winners, you become a better winner. If you hang around successful people, you get better at success. And if you hang around whining, thumb-sucking boneheads, you become a better whining, thumb-sucking bonehead."

Is Networking a Struggle?

Networking is not a struggle, not something you *have* to do, accomplish, or "put up with" as you get to where you are going. Rather, networking is something you "get to do," a blessing, a way to enjoy and to expand your sphere of influence. Inspired networking finds ways to give back to your community, your world, to meet so many creative people that it is actually a gift.

People who understand and are extremely effective at networking think of it as a skill. You learn how to politely break off a conversation and move on to the next person. You have your tools ready — business cards, brochures, etc. You realize your innate personal power, abilities, talents and gifts.

I have developed expertise in networking since 1997, and I have discovered it is more about the quality and effectiveness at being me, at you being you, at being a real, passionate and a focused individual. Life, business, your success with family, all of it is an "inside job." Improve what is going on "inside" and it changes what is really going on "outside."

For as I work harder on myself, on becoming a more enlightened person, then more enlightened people are naturally attracted to me. Grow who you are, and you grow your world, your connections, your prosperity, and all the wonderful things that will come into your life.

Networking is not only creating relationships, but digging deeper and creating true friendships with people who you not only want to do business with, but with people you want to have a beer with, have lunch with, spend time with because you really like them. If your goal is to make new friends, to help other people, to find common ground, then you will become one of the most skillful people in human communication — and is there really anything more important in business?

Plus the stories you hear will enhance your life.

Intentional and Purposeful Networking

"Forget about goal setting. It is all about goal getting." — Anonymous

Activity without purpose is like a one-legged duck swimming in a circle, a ship without a rudder or a feather in the wind. There is also a huge difference between activity and productivity.

Networking is not just an activity, but an action to get results. It is all about building and creating advocates. It is a way to pursue dreams and help others discover their dreams, too. It is not just about meeting someone new; you need to have a desire and an eye on accelerating the relationship, inventing new ways to help one another.

Everything that happens in your life is an intention. Create clearer intentions: Get the results you intend. Everyone you meet can add to or be a benefit. However, this benefit may not be realized or even understood for weeks, months or years.

Have goals, a list of desired outcomes. Who do you need to meet to get to the next level in your business? Who can help you? What organizations do you need to have an affiliation with? What do you need next? Who can help you find it? And be sure to ask those questions of your new connections and look for ways to help them accelerate to hypergrowth in their business.

And as Zig Ziglar put it so memorably, "You can get everything in life you want if you help enough other people get what they want." I say, find out how to help more and more people faster and faster, in more unique and interesting ways. Everyone appreciates that you are thinking about them, trying to help or connect them up with people who could be great resources for them to grow their companies. Believe that you may be just one connection away from huge strides in your business and personal growth.

Active participation is the key. Of course, caring for others, making friends, is the key element, but a dedication to networking that produces results should be your focus. This is the way to get what you want, and give others what they want faster. Use your time to create relationships with the purpose of creating inroads into new productivity.

Focused, results-based action plants the seeds that grow into beanstalks. Climb higher. Get the golden goose. Go. Do. Create. And most of all, stay inspired. Find better ways to stay and engage with this world with peak performance, with believing and achieving self-efficacy. Use your focused energy and you will experience unusual and wondrous adventures, and will find yourself in exciting situations and rewarding circumstances. With the right focus, magic does happen in ways you cannot imagine.

Do More Networking

This may be an obvious idea, but have you set a goal on how many networking events you will attend this week, this month? How many new people you wish to meet? How many new clients you want to get? Then this focused and goal approach to networking will get you the results you want.

Ask this question: How many people do this? Believe me, very, very few. Don't you want to stand out from the crowd? Then set these targets now. Do not wait until you finish another sentence. Find websites in your area, meetup groups, all kinds of new places to meet people, and you will be light years ahead of most people who merely say, "I guess I need to network more." **Again, do not network by default.**

Public speaking is one of people's most deep-seated fears. I say, find ways to do this more and you will enjoy it. You may even create a love for speaking in front of people. It is exactly the same with networking — practice. Do it more often. You will become an expert, get results and it will become second nature. You will thrive and excel because you do it, practice it and develop skills that you can use for a lifetime.

Occasionally, go network in unusual places, outside your normal circles, such as art fairs, metaphysical trade shows, auto shows, beer festivals, etc. Not only is it different, but it exposes you to different kinds of people and subcultures. You never know who you'll meet, or where you'll meet the next key person to have a huge impact on your business or your life.

As you find interesting places to network, be willing to pay for these opportunities. Some of the most dynamic and beneficial places to network charge fees. This is good. Why? Because these groups are professionally run and the people who join them are serious about getting results and serious about helping you get results.

I once joined the Denver Metro Chamber of Commerce and got an 1,100% return on my investment in 10 months. Do you think I cared it cost me money? Try investing in the stock market and getting an 1,100% return in 10 months.

I joined the Boulder Chamber and received a 7,000% return in seven months. So join chambers, trade shows, entrepreneurial groups, Rotary Clubs, as these are places to expand your connections.

But most importantly, choose carefully, for the shotgun approach doesn't work as well as committing to specific groups and organizations where you can really dig in. Put in the effort and it will pay off. And be dedicated to the group or organizations you join, for it is much better to dig deep than wide. Someone once told me, "Dig an inch wide and a mile deep."

Word-of Mouth: What is this, Really?

Have you ever said or heard someone say, "I get all my referrals by word-of-mouth." Are you one of those phenomenal business people who is so amazing at what you do that you're sure, any minute now, everyone in the entire country is going to pick up the phone and call you? How's that working for you?

To develop your business by only word-of-mouth is a fallacy. You can always amplify word-of-mouth. It doesn't just happen without you doing something. Networking is your skill set to accelerate word-of-mouth, to watch people correctly refer business to you, because you have explained to them how to do this. It isn't done just by default nor without your participation.

Let's say a client of yours, who is extremely loyal, likes who you are and what you do. They call you and say, "I have eight new people I just met who want to do business with you, and I gave them your card and they will be calling you next week." What is wrong with this scenario? Will they really call? Maybe, if you are lucky, one of the eight might call you.

What other step do you need? What information do you need to explain to this loyal client how to turn these connections into real solid new clients for your company? You need the contact information of these eight people. You then have control so you can follow up and contact them. This will amplify your word-of-mouth. Teach or explain to your loyal clients how to refer you, how to connect you with their names, cellphones and emails, and you will create a stream of referrals.

Learn more effective ways to connect people, especially so they both have each other's contact information. Do this and you will help people, not just pretend you are helping.

The Magic of Networking

"Leap and the net will appear."— Les Brown.

There is a magic going on once you decide to network — believe it works, and you get intensely involved.

Some people are adverse to reading business books, because they think they are boring. But when you dig, read authors such as Bob Procter and Brian Tracy, listen to Tony Robbins, Zig Ziglar, Les Brown, Jim Rohn and Jack Canfield, you begin to see they are inspiring you. There is magic in their words, ideas and ways of inspiring you to your own greatness. And when you are inspired with new ideas and new insights, you can move mountains and make massive changes in your world.

As you set an intention in your networking, you immediately begin moving toward that intention. And once you commit to the goal, the strangest thing begins to happen, according to Brian Tracy, at that exact time, your goal, your dream, your vision of what you want to create in your life begins racing toward you, too.

There is magic in getting around new people, new ideas, getting out of your isolated world, into a world of limitless opportunity. There is magic in beginning, in taking that first step into your dreams. There is adventure around the corner. There is an oscillation between the ordinary and the extraordinary, when you dare to dream it so, when you dare to believe it is possible, when the entrepreneurial spirit of pure creativity awakens within you and spawns innovation.

It is as if your destiny is being created and unfolding all at the same time. There is magic in action, in believing you can do a thing, anything, and that your networking efforts will put you in circumstances that propel you and inspire you to do more than you have yet accepted as possible.

Networking is getting new clients by creatively connecting the dots, putting yourself and others in situations that will help everyone. And when you take part, get involved, dig in, things begin to happen. People call out of the blue. Referrals come in the back door. Business accelerates. You jump-start a dream. Others start to see you "as a confident visionary." The phone rings and someone asks to know more about what you do. There is a momentum shift, as if the floodgates are opening, and you didn't even know there were any floodgates.

It is important in life, in all that we do, to leave room for the magical, for the unexpected, the inexplicable, the perplexing but wondrous ways that new business can appear. Now, I completely believe in tracking and measuring all your marketing, advertising and networking, for you do need to see what is effective.

However, you can't create magic if you just sit around and wait for the magic to happen. To accomplish your highest and dominant aspirations, in your drive to succeed, something mysterious, miraculous and magical is helping you, is aiding you. Have faith. Take action. Take a risk. Napoleon Hill calls this the work of infinite intelligence. I call it magic, or the divine nature of things. Call it whatever, but it is real. If you trust in it, it can influence and create results that you cannot even imagine.

But the key is to keep open, be aware, and have a heightened and acute sense of awareness to see the opportunities that arise, to witness the incredulous, to watch and wait for a chance, to become a business seer. When you are vitally involved in building a dream, watch for others to show up to help you. **"Whatever you can do, or dream you can, begin it. Boldness has genius, power and magic in it." — Goethe**

Have 100% faith in this magical and unexpected help, this idea that once you decide, and keep on deciding that nothing can stop you, that you are already successful. You just need time to catch up to it, believe that you cannot fail, that there is joy and bliss and adventure in what you do, then magic is inevitable. Things will happen in the most helpful and sometimes peculiar ways.

You will see what others don't quite see yet. You not only will create opportunities, but they also will begin to create themselves, and you will be racing toward these opportunities just as fast as they are racing toward you.

Embrace this added-value factor, and it will enhance your journey. Magic thrives within a beginner's mind. So have the sense of wonder of a 2-year-old, where everything is fresh, new and interesting. Tap into esoteric and unseen parts of what can be, what already is and what has been, and let the magic show up and begin to happen in the most exciting ways.

The #1 Way to Be Effective in Networking

"Hello! You play to win the game." — Herm Edwards

What would you guess is the No. 1 way to be an effective networker? Would you say it's being able to speak in front of a group? Good answer, but not the one I'm looking for. Maybe improved communication overall would do the trick? Also, vital in networking, but again not quite it. How about to be extremely effective in networking, you must invest time in others or help others first? Both excellent answers, but not the answer I am looking for.

Since 1997, I've been running my own networking business and thinking a lot about how to improve this skill. I have to say the best way to ensure you will be effective in networking **is to be absolutely great at being you**. This means being so on fire, so passionate, so focused on the direction you are going that nothing can stop you. In fact, you must believe and feel that you are unstoppable in everything that you do.

Take time to form clear, concise, vivid dreams, goals and aspirations. Put in the daily effort, no excuses, to realize these dreams. Be 100%, not 99%, but 100% committed to your success. When you have this level of drive and passion, you can achieve anything.

I'm not committed to your dreams. You are. Other people will not do it for you. You do it. Not one ounce of your success is given to you by someone else. You make it happen. You take 100% responsibility to create the life you want. With this applied energy, other like-minded people will show up to help. But you must be the catalyst.

According to Larry Winget, best-selling author and speaker, "Success is your own damn fault."

Can this level of commitment be taught? No. You just choose it. Success, your success, is a decision. Decide, and this decision is how you will accomplish anything you desire, so all things will align and magic will happen. Your effectiveness is proportional to your own belief in yourself.

Believe in your talents and abilities to achieve what you deeply want and it begins to happen. Other people's confidence in you means nothing, if you don't believe in yourself.

And you may say, "Of course I believe in myself. That is obvious." But is there a modicum of doubt that sometimes creeps into your mind, which is limiting you and your peak performance, a little insecurity holding you back from creating what you want?

Look carefully at every thought you think, every belief you have. Get better and better at being the powerful person you really are and you will attract the right people to help you. We can all become more effective at who we are.

21 Networking Don'ts!

Humorous Taboos, Faux Pas, Things That Don't Work in Networking

Sometimes the best way to explain something clearly is to define its opposite or contrast, and what it is not.

1) Never stand up to talk in front of a crowd with your zipper down. Seriously, I once had a speaker do this at a networking group in front of about 20 people. It was memorable, humorous, and I never forgot this person. Still not one I would do.

2) Don't ramble when speaking in front of a group. You may not even notice you are doing this, but others do. Talking too much can bore people to death, and it's usually not a good way to attract the right people. Most won't care to meet you later, won't take your phone calls because they know you will take up too much of their time as you ramble on and on.

   No rambling also applies to the phone. I bet you know people who you are hesitant to call, or to take their calls, because you know they will talk and talk and waste your time. As Dale Carnegie said, "Be clear, be brief and be seated."

3) When talking in front of a group, don't look at only one side of the room or at a single person. Scan everyone. If you look at one person only, it not only makes that person uncomfortable, but the other people you are talking to begin to tune you out. Again, scan the room. Talk to everyone in the group. Believe you are interesting and that you have something valuable to say to everyone. This belief alone usually holds and keeps their attention. Strive to inform and inspire.
4) Don't stand hunched over, with bad posture. Don't be monotone, lethargic, languid and bittersweet. If you are not excited, inspiring and compelling, find a way to become better at your delivery. Join Toastmasters. Effective body language, intonations and voice inflections get people's attention. Being boring is the death of public speaking.
5) Don't start your speech with an exclamation that you are not good at public speaking. They'll probably figure that out all by themselves. Humor

here, right? Instead, be bold; be willing to be mediocre speaking in front of people initially until you do it enough times that you become exceptional. Believe you have important things to say and say it with enthusiasm. Do this and people will believe, and be influenced that what you are saying is powerful. Be enthusiastic, but don't get so intoxicated with your own enthusiasm, and your own ideas, that you forget to look around to see if the crowd is responding in a positive way also.

6) Don't appear to be distracted or preoccupied. Especially when talking to a single person, give them your full attention, full eye contact, undivided attention. Act as if this one conversation is more important than anything else you could be doing. Do this especially with your loved ones. Watch the difference. This complete attention on them, on what they are saying, is huge in creating relationships and really valuing who people are.

As the late Earl Nightingale once said, "Treat everyone as if they are the most important person on Earth." "Treat everyone as if they are a million-dollar client." — Brian Tracy. This will make you incredibly effective.

7) Don't ever take a phone call in a meeting unless it is an emergency. Briefly tell the person you are talking to that it is an emergency, and excuse yourself and leave the room. It will take just a moment. Phones have voicemail. If the call is important, I bet they will leave a message. Never take a second call when you are on the phone with someone else. The call-waiting feature is to notify you, not to interrupt you or who you are talking with right now. Again, this is impolite. It annoys people and shows disrespect.
8) Don't sit down when addressing a small group. Stand up. Do something unique, such as walk around the room or use a prop or two, or sit on the back of your chair. Anything you can do to be different. Be bold. Be audacious. Be interesting and intriguing. You will be remembered.

Effective networking is to be remembered and to make a positive impression. Remember this: You are extremely creative whether you believe it or not. According to Brian Tracy, "Statistics prove that children up to the age of 6 are usually in the top 5% of the most creative. After that age, they are in the lower 5%." Why? Someone convinced them that they were not creative. Get your creative swagger back. Engage your creativity — be entertaining.

9) Don't be boring, ordinary or unwilling to use your entire arsenal of weapons to defeat mediocrity. Instead, believe you are a master communicator. Use inflection in your voice, change tone, speed and volume. Energize your body language. Add the element of surprise. Inspire others with new ideas, especially about your specific industry.

This establishes your expert status.

Take a moment to uncover things you know that you may take for granted, then repackage, repurpose those ideas in new ways. When you are an expert in a certain field, often you may think everyone knows the most obvious facts or ideas, but usually they don't. According to Bob Berg, ask someone who is not an expert in your field what 10 things they would like to know about your field of knowledge. They just may be things you think everyone already knows. Plus, you can always put your own spin on something people already know to remind them or refresh them with a new angle. Don't, however, be the kind of person who has an uncanny grasp of the obvious. Use language to intrigue and to inspire, not as a sedative. No one wants to listen to someone who tells them things they already know, who tells them things that are so mundane and obvious it only makes them want to run away. Life is about discovering new ideas, new ways of doing things, ways to get better. As you discover new things that inspire you, then find creative ways to express those ideas, find a fresh approach. People love the unique, the exceptional and the creative. You are creative. Just turn on that creative faucet more often, so it doesn't rust. Do this and people will listen. Practice what you have to say. Of course, you want to be prepared. But believe you are talented enough to also be improvisational. Be spontaneous. Bob Bennett, who was in Toastmasters for 10 years, told me, "To be phenomenal at public speaking, it is 90% who you are, and 10% the skills you have learned." "Don't be afraid to go out on a limb. That's where the fruit is," said Will Rogers.

It is OK to stand out, to be different, to get people's attention, to interrupt the ordinary, to impress, to take a chance, to do things that no one else is doing. You can achieve nothing great without taking risks. Risk is the way you get out of your comfort zone, into new territories, find new ideas, invent new products. There are always ways to get better results. Do something new.

Once at a chamber of commerce after-hours event, I met a magician. I asked if he had a card and he pulled out his wallet, opened it up and it caught on fire: Memorable! Always ask yourself, "Is there a better, more effective, more interesting way to do what I have always done?" "Creativity is thinking up new things. Innovation is doing new things." — Theodore Levitt.

10) Don't dress sloppy or show up unkempt or disheveled. There are no casual dress days in networking. According to Jim Rohn, "Casualness

creates casualties." Polish your shoes. Go spend some money on updated and fashionable clothes. Dress for success. If you look great, you will feel great. This energy will transfer to who you are talking to. You will make a great impression. Believe you are successful. Dress that way. Act that way. Let your reputation precede you. It makes you feel great when you look absolutely your best. People notice. People will notice that you are meticulous and that you are a cut above those who are too casual, or do not take time to look professional.

11) Don't keep the spotlight on yourself too long. Put the spotlight on others by using quotes, testimonials, praising others, asking questions about others. Say nice things about other people.

Never, ever, ever, say bad or negative things about someone else. Why not? Well, if I say something negative about someone else, the person I am talking to may listen, but they also may think I will say something negative about them when they aren't around.

Sure you want people to know what you do, and that you are an expert in your field, but you really want people to know that you care, that you are concerned and you understand what they do, what they are going through, their business, their struggles. Do this and people will want to help you too.

Again, be polite and care, put the spotlight on them. This is one of the most important things any of us can do in all our relationships. One of the best ways to do this is use words like, "thank you" and "please" and "you're welcome." Brian Tracy said that when speaking in any foreign country, one of the first phrases he would learn would be thank you in their language.

12) Be credible. Don't stretch the truth to fit your agenda. It is vital to impress others, to be eloquent, but not with exaggeration. Be someone people not only believe but someone they also believe in.

Be the person who not only speaks the truth, but when you speak, make it ring true. When something is true, people get it, feel it and sense it. This urges and inspires them to take action, to do more than they even have thought they can do. Do this and you will influence and get others to be part of your vision.

13) This may be the biggest one: Don't criticize, argue, disagree, act irritable or be rude. Remember, "Tact is the intelligence of the heart" (source unknown). So never say negative things about your competition or criticize a company, another organization or person. Be mindful of not only what you say out loud, but also what you think inwardly.

    Sure, you may be excellent in being positive around a crowd, but when you're around confidants or people in your inner circle, do you go on tirades, talk badly or criticize other people? Never do this. Instead, be a positive force for good. Do this (outwardly and inwardly) and you will have a tremendous effect on your world and the people you surround yourself with. Brian Tracy once said, "Never criticize anyone for anything."

14) Don't be crude. Never be too controversial or do things out of bad taste. It is OK to be humorous, to step out of the accepted norms, but walk the line of propriety and correctness. People love a good joke, but maybe not a tasteless or an ethnic one. Find ways to push the envelope without offending others or being so controversial that others are repelled.

Everyone is part of a subculture. It is easy to inadvertently offend them, so be careful how you package your message, how you entertain to make a point. This is the lost art of tact and chivalry.

15) Don't be so selfish, self-serving, self-consumed or self-absorbed that you forget to help others. Be kind, considerate and empathetic. Most people want to know how you can help them, what's in it for them, how what you do can fit in with what they want. Find the need in others, and support and strengthen that need. Give a helping hand and others will lend a hand, too. Give and you will find that you get back in the most unusual and unexpected ways. As someone once said, "If you walk a mile in someone else's shoes, you are a

mile away and have a new pair of shoes." And it is OK to have some fun. Banter is usually a sign of friendship and a deeper relationship, too.

16) Don't emotionally dump on people. Make a conscious effort not to speak of negative things or personal hardships unless they are great stories with an incredible lesson or an uplifting message of triumph. People want to be inspired. They want hope, ideas and information that solve problems, that gets them to take focused action. People want to be around others who are going somewhere, people who are on a mission, who are excited, motivated and can push them beyond their own unrealized limitations. Misery may love company, but you do not have to be part of that company. If you want hang out with people who habitually complain, use excuses or criticize others, *you will never achieve your dreams.* Be very careful who you spend a lot of time around. Believe, even if you must be around them that you have the personal power not to let their negativity affect you.

17) Don't tell people what is not possible; inspire them to do the impossible. As Walt Disney once said, "It is always fun to do the impossible." In fact, awhile ago I was in Disneyland during the Christmas holiday with, at the time, my 3-year-old daughter. It was dark, late evening, and I was holding her hand. We were standing in front of the famous Disneyland castle, completely decorated in white lights as fireworks exploded in the sky. We were right in front of the bronze statue of Walt Disney holding Mickey Mouse's hand. And as the fireworks lit up the sky and the music filled all of Disneyland, I got tears in my eyes as the song simply played: "Believe." Believe and all your dreams can come true."
18) Don't be late, not a single minute. The first and most important step to master your time is to always, always be on time for everything. In other words, discipline yourself. Master yourself and you will become a master of time management. Even better be 10 or 15 minutes early. When you show up late to an appointment, a meeting, anywhere you are supposed to be, it basically says

to others, “My time is more important than yours.” Everyone has real reasons (excuses) why they are constantly late. Stop making those excuses. Be on time (or early) to everything, and this quality will create credibility with everyone you meet.

According to Brian Tracy, continually ask yourself this question: “What is the most valuable use of my time right now?” Do this and you will be on time. Do this and you will not waste other people’s time. Do this and you will be so focused that you will accomplish more than almost everyone you know. “Master yourself, and you master time.”

Being on time shows respect for others and that you are a conscientious person. It also shows (by your actions) that you are dependable and will do what you say you are going to do.

In business and in networking, this learned time-management skill is huge. Use it as a great character trait. Caring about someone else’s time, acknowledging that others are busy and have things to do, too, is a great habit to develop. If occasionally, you are late, apologize and take full responsibility. For as Benjamin Franklin once said, "Do not ruin an apology with an excuse." I was late because there was so much traffic. Don't even go there.

19) Don't appear sad, depressed, down, negative, angry, irritable, a braggart, a know it all, or anything else negative. These traits may attract people to you, but will not attract the right people to you. If you feel down, stop what you are doing and take some time to reconnect with yourself and who you are. Go walk in nature. Get more sleep. Eat better foods. Re-focus on your goals. Read inspiring books. Get around successful and positive people. Whatever is going on inside of you is what you project to the outside world; it is also what you begin seeing in your outer world. Clean up your inner world, and you will be crystal-clear in what you project. If you are not excited, motivated, thinking creative and positive thoughts, feeling positive, then do whatever you need to do to change that. Take a mini-vacation. Take time for yourself.

But most important, be careful what you think. “Don’t believe everything you … believe.” Be aware of limiting beliefs you let run around in your head. This ultimately is the secret of being a master in the field of networking and a master of yourself. Continually remind yourself of all the things (you know) that are the right things to do and to say, so you don’t slide into that comfort zone of mediocrity, inaction and apathy.

On occasion, you may share with others some difficulties you are going through; these hardships can create a sense of trust with others. Just don’t do this all the time and get a reputation for complaining and talking about all the negatives and what is not possible. As Joe Peanuts, dang near cowboy poet, once said, “Complain when yer dead.”

It is your job to become more effective at who you are. Be so focused, so energetic that everyone you meet enjoys being around you. Do it now. Don’t do the things that you know repel excited people. Do positive and exciting things that add great energy to you, your life and the lives of others and you will be massively successful in networking. But more so, you will be absolutely successful in life.

20) This actually happened in one of our referral meetings: Never fall asleep in a networking luncheon. Not sure why, but you get very few connections and people begin to talk.

21) Don't believe networking won't work for you. This is the worst, most self-fulfilling prophecy that you do not want to fulfill.

The Difference Between Elocution and Execution

"Be so good at what you do, they can't ignore you." — Steve Martin

In networking, it should be your goal to find more creative ways to help more and more people. Don't just talk about this — do it. Make it a daily routine. Write it out on a piece of paper who will I meet and help this week.

Networking is about helping people. Give first, get later. "Networking is creating opportunities for other people that weren't there before." Sure you know this, but are you executing, are you doing it, are you really taking the time with people? Or are you using the excuse of being too busy, or I will meet with my favorite people, the new people, the people who are important to me, some day?

Create new clients and new connections for people now. Always keep in mind how to help, what you can do to give, how to encourage, how to be more supportive. Then what happens next is easy:

Rewards, fun, inspiration and loyalty. This is easy to do, with a kind word in an email, or left on a voice mail, or saying you have a really great referral or connection for them.

Networking is about people; it is about being in the people business. Many years ago, Charles Schwab once said he would pay more for this skill in America than any other skill: "The ability to get along with other people." There is a fine line between tact and justifying bad behavior.

And a note: Give selflessly, without expecting anything in return. And other people will get it, on a gut level. Be there for people, a friend, someone who listens, a person who is continually finding new and creative ways to give back, to connect, to introduce people to the right connections who can help.

Networking is about inciting inspiration, adding a modicum of peace to all that you do, adding enthusiasm, and creating deep relationships with the people you like. Then you attract the right people, the right organizations, the right circumstances to help you flourish in your own life.

The right action in networking (where to place your attention) is on discovering new and inventive ways to produce results for others, for people you trust and respect, people you would refer your own mother or brother to if they needed that service or product. When you put emphasis on other's needs, you will have no choice but to reap the rewards.

Follow Up, Follow Through and Follow Up Again

I once met a woman who couldn't remember any of the 60 people she met at a networking event. I told her, "When at an event, after you speak with someone you would like to follow up with, write a little note on the back of their business card, or in your notebook, say that Joe has a son who is in Saudi Arabia, or whatever was important that you talked about. This will trigger you to remember Joe and what he does, so when you call back, you can pick up where you left off from the previous conversation. It is a simple technique but extremely effective."

Also, if you follow up quickly, let's say in the next 24 hours, you will remember a lot of the people you talked to. One main issue with networking is that many people do not follow up at all. And most people will not call or email you back when you do follow up with them.

Do not let this discourage you. Sometime you need to look at it as a numbers game. Keep working your connections and keep following up with people until, in your heart, you know this really is a waste of time or not worth the emailing or calling them again. Sometime the best word to learn is "next."

Though following up is the key to your networking success, for if you don't follow up with people, you can't get the benefits: No new clients, no new resources, no new friends. All you end up with is a stack of business cards.

Think for a moment, what if that business card becomes a new client, a new connection that turns into a long-term relationship? How much is that worth to you and your company? What if that client becomes a power partner or referral partner and refers 50 new clients to you? How valuable can that really be?

Follow up and believe it is not only a numbers game, but also that every single person you meet can be of value to you and you can be of value to them.

When calling and following up with anyone, believe that you are not bothering them, but rather, believe that this could be one of the most important conversations they ever have had.

This is a huge example: I had a person who sold health insurance. He contacted a woman he had met. She didn't have health insurance. Soon she signed up for health insurance. Two weeks later, she was diagnosed with breast cancer. Do you think she was glad he had followed up with her? She did go through cancer treatment, had surgery and is doing fine, by the way.

Follow Up Quickly

24 hours is best, 48 hours is acceptable. If it is later than that, do it anyway. A question: "What impresses successful people and annoys everyone else? Consistent and persistent following up." Do this because that is what successful people like and expect.

Be sure they remember you. I think the best way to be remembered is to be fully present and attentive. To be so much who you are, with such a presence that people are impressed at the way you communicate, listen, use humor and do something unique. Believe everyone you meet is also important, impressive and has a lot to offer you, too. You will find common ground, interesting things to talk about. Give them your full attention, and really see if you can find something in common, some ways to help each other. This will be memorable.

I met a woman at a networking event. She was born and raised in Colorado, like me. She was in a health products and service company and had lost 30 pounds. I told her I had just lost 12 pounds. I told her I knew someone who could really use her services. Guess what? When I called her back, she remembered me.

Tell Them You'll Follow Up

I usually tell people, "I will follow up, because that is what I do." Try this: I went to a seminar by David Behr, a sales trainer for many years. He said when you do follow up, in the first words in an email or when leaving a voice message on the phone, say, "As promised," as this is effective and also often gets them to call you and follow up.

When meeting someone at a networking event, tell them you may have a connection or something that can help them. Also, when at a networking event, use the broad-stroke approach: Meaning, think about every person you meet as not only a great connection for you, but also a great connection for others you know as well, so you can introduce them later and both will benefit.

I met a woman who did loyalty programs for restaurants and retail, and I met another person who owned a coffee shop, so I connected them both and they were delighted to meet each other.

Continually scan your mind, the people you know, and watch how these connections can help them all. Be known as a connector. This gets people's attention. Believe you are a great connector, and that you can connect the dots in ways that are creative, helpful, that will create business that was never there before. Believe this and you begin doing it.

It really is better to get than to give a business card. Many times I see people at networking events hand out a lot of cards and brochures, as if this is effective networking. It isn't. They just may be a self-serving person who is out there to hand out a ton of cards and promote themselves.

When you get a business card or a phone number from someone, you have control of the follow up, and you can add them to your database if you ask their permission. If you will discipline yourself to follow up quickly, you will get unexpected results in networking.

Just don't be discouraged if some people do not respond. I met a very young entrepreneur who told me, "No one will call me back, and no one can afford or will pay for my service."

I asked him, how many people did he meet or contact. He said, "10." I said try 100, or 1,000. Don't mentally give up after 10 tries. That is not the way business, networking or getting results happens. "Following up is vital, following through and doing what you said you will do is paramount."

Use a Database

Use some form of contact-management system. In networking, in sales, in business, nothing is as important as creating a usable database. Your database is your gold mine. It is the most valuable asset you have, so acquire and keep building.

You can't be effective at follow up if you meet hundreds of people and list them in a notebook or have business cards strewn all over the place. To be effective in networking, use a good database program. Find a program or way to keep track of all the people you have met. Find one you can use to send emails and track the history of your conversations. This means you can log each contact by noting it in the database, and have a place for a personal note.

I met Joe at our local chamber and he is going to Saudi Arabia next week. I'll call him at the end of March, and ask, "How was your trip?"

Find a program that also has a feature to schedule callbacks and remind you to do them. At 10a, you'll get a reminder on your computer or cell that says, "Call back Joe Thursday morning at 10a." With the speed and changes in technology, find or search on the Internet for a program that meets your needs and expands your database. The most valuable part of your business, your gold mine, is your current and updated, sorted and qualified database. Do not take this lightly or overlook the importance of keeping a current and usable database. If you do not, people and contacts and connections will fall through the cracks and you won't even be aware of this.

Schedule Regular Times To Do Follow-up Calls

The number of new contacts you get can be overwhelming, so it's vital to set a time each day to make calls — say before 9:30a or after 4p every day for an hour or so. When you call new people, enter their information into the database, one at a time as you complete each call. "This is easy to do but, also, easy not to do," as Jeff Olsen said in his world-famous book, "A Slight Edge." This may be one of the most profound concepts not just in networking or business, but also in life. Think about how it applies to almost everything you do.

You also can add some of these contacts into your laptop after hours as you watch TV or when you are at the kitchen table. You don't have to put in every single bit of information, just name, company name, phone number, email, and where you met them or where the referral came from. One idea is to find someone you can pay to enter the information. This is usually a minor expense for the value you get. Set goals on how many people you will add to your database in one month, two, three months, in an entire year. Most cellphones can scan a business card now and add it to your database.

In your database, create groups, warm clients, from this chamber, from that networking event and so on. If you do a little every day, if you set goals on the number of people you want to meet weekly, or at a particular event, if you have a plan on how to follow up with these connections, you will be massively, did I say, MASSIVELY more successful than most who do networking and get nominal results by default. Which brings up one more point: Take this massive, focused and productive action. I guarantee, you can do more, you can be more productive. "Do it today. Action is king."

You also can follow up with people by email, or send them a card, or with a large client, a shoe in a Fed Ex package with a note, "Just wanted to get a foot in the door." Get creative. If it is a particularly huge client or important connection you need to make, use your creativity, put in the effort and follow up in some unique way.

Set the number of times you will follow up before you give up, say I will contact that person eight times, and if they don't respond, send a last-attempt call to action. Usually on my last attempt I say or type in an email or text, "At this stage I feel like I am bugging you, so if you want I will let you call me back." Very often they will respond to this.

And if I don't hear back, I will take them out of my database. Some people, those tenacious rebels, never give up until someone says stop contacting me. This is a judgment call. Just don't give up too easily. People are busy. A week from now might be just the right time to talk, connect or set up a meeting.

You Don't Have To Follow Up With Everyone

I usually do not like to delve into the negative, but it might be appropriate here. If you meet someone at an event who is not very nice, cold, curt, not at all wanting to communicate much, I personally would not follow up with them. There are too many caring, kind and considerate people in the world, so don't waste your time on people who, on a gut level, you know don't feel right. I call them "Bingo Brains."

Just shake off their negative energy, and go find good-as-gold people and follow up with them. Do this and you will have fun. And fun is really the best way to do business, and grow your company and get phenomenal results in your marketing. According to Dang Near Cowboy poet Joe Peanuts, "If you ain't havin' fun yer probably goin' in the wrong direction." Or, to paraphrase Zig Ziglar, "If you meet someone rude, that's good. It means you are working hard. In fact, there are only about nine of these people out there anyway; they just move around a lot." So you probably won't meet another rude person for quite awhile.

Use your intuition and common sense here. You know people who have high energy, who are successful, who are excited about what they do. These are the people who you want to help and get to know you. Most successful and highly effective people are nice, willing to talk, to help, and are usually very humble.

But also be careful to not prejudge people too quickly. You might meet someone who is having a bad day, or is in a crisis that day, didn't sleep well and tomorrow they will seem to be a completely different person.

Have Something to Offer

This is a vital habit to create when following up with people you have recently met. Always try to give something back. When I call people I just met within 24 hours, and I hit their voice mail, instead of asking them for something, I find creative ways to leave something of value for them. People are inundated with sales calls; make yours different. "I just met you at the networking event and I know you cater events. My company does many events every year, and I would like to discuss an event I may be doing soon."

Be sincere and truthful, but also see how you can help people get new connections, new clients, new ideas that will help them too. Do this as a habit, and you will excel in your networking efforts.

Email Follow-up Techniques

Let's say you want to contact people first by email. That's OK. I usually will send an email again within 24 hours, (but again, if you take 48 or 72 hours or a week, follow up anyway) and put something personal in the subject line.

Here is an excellent idea I have created: I usually put their phone number in the subject line. No one ever does this and it gets their attention immediately.

It is vital to call the next day, if they haven't responded, and say you emailed them yesterday, wondering if they received it. A variation on this is to call a person you just met within 24 to 48 hours, and if you hit voice mail, then send an email. In the subject line put in their phone number and say, I just left you a voice message on this number. The double benefit of doing this is that their contact information is right there in the subject line so its information doesn't fall through the cracks.

Again, be creative. Come up with your own ideas. Split test marketing ideas. Find interesting ways to get people's attention. It is like throwing a brick through a plate-glass window. People are so overwhelmed with stimuli, when something new comes into their awareness, it is refreshing and an effective first contact for you.

OK, so you don't really throw bricks, but do something unique and your efforts will leave an impression. Marketing is getting through their filters, instead of the ordinary ways so many people try to get their attention.

Do something different, sincere and for the reason of creating a relationship. But most importantly, do not give up. Take massive action. Send out 50 emails instead of just a couple a day. Usually I send out 200 emails on my prospecting Monday. You will get a percentage of people to call you back and you will get momentum, and "momentum is earned."

Mining For Gold

"Do some gold calling."— Chellie Campbell from her book, *The Wealthy Spirit*

When you follow up with people, it's like you're an old prospector in 1849 digging in the biggest gold mine ever discovered in California, and you are the only one who knows where it's at. Each follow-up call you make can lead to a relationship, a new client, a valued friend, a referral, just like an untapped, yet undiscovered gold mine or an endless chain of referrals: It is your fortune being built.

The Long-Term Value of a Single Client

Let's say you sell a product or service that costs $500, and that product is bought annually by your customer. Say they reorder, buy again, for 10 years. That is $5,000. Now say you have other products, and they buy another $2,000 of more services or products from you. Then let's say they really value and appreciate what you do and refer 10 new clients who do the same, spend $7,000 for the next 10 years. That is $77,000 from a single connection, a single call, a single follow up.

Making one sale, that follow-up call, getting one new client can be incredible, and can result into thousands and thousands of dollars over the long term. So always think of the long-term value of a single, great client.

Now, realize how important that good-as-gold client can be. Your clients are your gold mine. And the gold never will run out as long as you treat them with care, appreciate them and value them not only as generating more money for you and your company, but also for being important people in the growth of your business, so continually find creative and better ways to appreciate and serve them.

Tell Me Something I Don't Know

Did you know that volcanoes erupt all the time on Neptune? Volcanoes that are miles high, bigger than any volcanoes ever seen on Earth. But, and this is a big but, it is so cold on Neptune, these volcanoes spew pure nitrogen, ice volcanoes, silver and frozen, shooting nitrogen miles into the frigid skies. So, I might've told you something you didn't know. OK, so this isn't about networking, but mix it up, be compelling.

My dear mother, Barbara, who is no longer around, lost her many years ago, always would say things that were so obvious. It was actually cute coming from my mother. I always told her that, "Mom, you have such an uncanny grasp of the obvious." So now when someone says something really obvious, I say, "I understand, Barbara," and they just look at me like "What?" Then I explain about my mother.

No one really likes to be told the obvious or to do something they were just about going to do anyway. Be flexible, unexpected, intriguing. You are creative, no matter what you believe. Just find ways to use that creativity.

Entrepreneurs are not crazy, wild people thinking only about making more and more money, but rather crazy, wild people thinking about and creating more and more value, seeing what others have not yet seen. They are people willing to take action on their dreams and ideas, their unwavering hopes, and they find ways to use failure and adversity as opportunities. Or as Thomas J. Watson, founder of IBM, might be paraphrased, "If you want to increase your success rate, double your failure rate." You can never really fail unless you give up.

To paraphrase Michael Gerber, in his world-famous book, "The E-Myth": "The people who do the best in business do so not because of what they know, but because of their insatiable desire to know more."

Take yourself out of beta mode, out of autopilot living, getting ready to get ready, and get into effective and intentional living. Learn from books, audio and video programs, from people, from observation, from using and stretching your imagination. "Life is learning, all else is commentary."

In networking, be intriguing, be compelling, be the light on a cloudy day, be anything but boring. Don't explain in detail the blatantly obvious. If you bore people, if you have an uncanny grasp of the obvious, if you are stuck in the automatons of the ordinary and mediocre, you will not attract the people and the circumstances you want. Instead, you actually will repel the people who could become advocates for what you do.

Find better ways to be interesting, to explain new ideas, information that others are not aware of. Find ways to relate this information in an interesting way, in stories, in parables, in new spins, in examples, results and testimonials, and you will become an asset to others you meet. You will become valuable rather than someone who is footnoting the obvious and just likes to hear themselves talk.

And yet, you can also say something everyone knows, repackage it, remind them of it in such a way as to stop them, interrupt them, get their complete attention. Have enough charisma so they remember you and become attracted to you, your business and help you with your visions and dreams.

There once was a mule that would not move. No matter what the owner did, it would just stand steadfast and refuse to budge. Finally the owner, with his son watching, hit the mule between the eyes with an eight-foot-long two-by-four. The mule reeled and went running around the corral, heehawing and kicking. The boy cried out, "Why did you do that?" The father calmly replied, "Just wanted to get that mule's attention."

But what can you do to get people's attention? People have their own agendas, problems and concerns, so why should they listen to you?

First, throw that brick through the plate-glass window of their perceptions, then say something fresh and compelling. It is your job in networking to not only be a good listener but also to be someone worth listening to, by speaking about things they do not know, or by being so engaging, so deep, so real that they can't ignore you.

There is an abundance of overused clichés, such as: A bird in the hand is worth two in the bush. The early bird gets the worm. A penny saved … no pain, no gain … on and on. Use your inventive mind, and maybe take an old, trite idea and freshen it up, put a new spin on an old cliché, like, "Let's come to that bridge when we cross it," or "I will see it when I believe it."

You can be unorthodox. You need to know if you are saying the same things over and over, if you are boring, if you are simply infatuated with your own ideas or stuck in the low drone of your own voice. It's a good idea to have someone videotape you speaking at a networking event. Then watch it. You will see places to improve.

There are more than 800,000 words in the English language and there are new ones being added daily. Learn more than 20. Add a new, colorful word to your vocabulary every day, at least every week, and you will have serendipity on your side. This will get you noticed in the world of communication, a person who knows the value of words, of becoming better at networking, speaking, entertaining.

Networking is a way of life. Networking is the universal language. Everyone wants to have more friends, better relationships, and more people they care about to hang out with. And if they don‘t, it is their way of hiding from life, living in fear and cynicism, and forgetting what is really important.

So be good at communication. Be good at understanding and find ways to have all the rough edges of your personality sanded smooth. Don’t be so prickly. Be nice. Enjoy life, for this is not just networking, but getting better at who you are and getting better at life.

You have the entrepreneurial spirit in you to design the life you want. There is and always will be the indomitable spirit of humanity in you. Let it out. Get in touch with it and create a life that you see beginning to form in your imagination.

Plus, you have many people in your client base who want to help you. They just need you to help amplify the process. There are many things you can do to amplify the referral process by being informed, educated and up to date with new ideas that can help people get more out of business.

For example, the other day I was listening to some introductory audio programs by a once-nationwide marketing and fulfillment company. They said exceptional marketing should interrupt, engage, educate and offer. And also, they said no one is really doing it. The giant companies, such as McDonalds, Pepsi and Budweiser, are just being creative, meaning interrupting you, getting you out of the alpha mode (unconscious, or autopilot mode) into the beta mode (where you are aware and conscious of the advertisement).

Then they use repetition, over and over to imbed and brand their products into your mind. This, by the way, takes millions of dollars. McDonalds marketing budget is in the billions. Most companies do not have that much to spend on branding.

With small businesses, use this "other" marketing system of interrupting, engaging, educating and offering, and you set yourself apart from all your competitors.

Again, tell people things they do not know. Engage them. Be a magnet for ideas, innovations and new information. This will put you in an entirely different category when networking and meeting, talking and expanding your already loyal relationships.

Get into a higher awareness. Learn, conjugate the world differently with new knowledge and you will attract the right people to you.

Find better ways to uncover ideas, the information that others are not aware of.

Here Is Something Different

Caught outside the darkness of your own ordinary mediocrity, where the sun is but a shot in the dark, where the stars shine out of order, there is an awakening of your deepest passions that adds a touch of magic to the mystery, living this high adventure, where you, instead, get caught in this exhilaration of speeding down the road of tomorrow with your imagination, pedal to the metal, at full throttle.

Guess what? You really do get to design your very own destiny.

Acknowledge People NOW!

"If you can't say something nice…."
— Your Mother!

Finding creative ways to acknowledge people for anything they do is a vital component in networking. The more you make this a habit, the more you foster goodwill, and the more you will become superior in business.

Make it a habit. Even when you leave someone a voice message or send them an email, say something uplifting and kind. Sure you know this is important, but are you doing it every day, consistently, no matter how you feel?

As you become superior, great, an over-the-top kind of person, you create a flood of referrals, of friendships, and business becomes a pleasure, not a grind. You get to work with only the powerful people who you like. And this is a huge key point, when you are self-employed, or working for yourself (and according to Brian Tracy, everyone is, and owns their own personal services business): You get to choose who you want to work with. Work with good people, those who you really like, and your business will thrive. In order to expand your business faster, spend more of your time with positive, uplifting and passionate people.

So acknowledge the people who are family, in your inner circle, and watch your personal relationships also bloom, grow and flourish. When you acknowledge others, they will want to help you, to do nice things for you, too. Edify, edify and edify.

Acknowledging others will inspire them to become and do more than they think they can. This is a way to inspire a higher form of action (right action), to engage people, to give hope, and to acknowledge that they are humans living a higher purpose.

Make it a consistent habit to send personal cards and notes, make appreciative phone calls, even if it's small acts of kindness, "Hey, that was a great meeting." "Thanks for getting that report done on time." "I really appreciate that referral you gave me." Whatever, just find the good and reward it, note it. Find ways to be grateful and appreciative, and you will create a movement. You will get many people going in the same direction, a positive conspiracy where good things are being done in your favor. Everyone is on your side. Everyone wants to find ways to help you.

Try it for a day, a month, six months, and see what results will happen. Track the effectiveness of this well-placed kindness, giving, caring and acknowledging the small and great things others do. Make it a conscious habit to catch people in the act of doing something amazing.

These ideas, small favors, ways to be kind, "are very easy to do, but they are also very easy not to do." There is that concept again that can really change everything.

Consistency and habit, the right attitude and good energy can move your life toward amazing results. Take time to say things to encourage people. Be real in your appreciation and you will change the world.

What else is there left to do? People have struggles, have difficulties, and seldom receive real praise or encouragement. **Everyone is fighting the**

good fight. Catch people doing good, show gratitude to others and you create an army of help on your side.

Do this and you become a master networker, but better than that, you become a master at life and how to live internally and externally in this world. When you are a force for good, a positive influence on others, on yourself, you can change minds, change attitudes and change the very course of your own world.

Be Fully Engaged

"Tug on anything at all and you'll find it connected to everything else in the universe." — John Muir

What are master communicators like? What are their traits? Are they people who just talk and talk, outgoing, those rare few who are always comfortable in any group? Maybe not. The most effective people in networking are the ones who are not only interesting and eloquent, but also those who are interested. So practice the fine art of *being interested.*

What should you be interested in? Be interested in what others have to say, but also in life, in what is going on, in the nuances of ideas, ideologies, in getting better and better at what you do, in what you think, in learning from others. Jim Rohn was famous for saying, "Never miss a thing."

Don't miss the magic, the mystery and the wonder of life, for it is a gift and an adventure. Find ways to heighten your own awareness, to notice everything, to never miss a thing. Increase your, "Spectrum of Consciousness" — a book by Ken Wilbur.

Think of everyone you meet as a learning interaction, and you do have the opportunity to gain insights from them. No matter how much you know, people know stuff you don't know. Be completely interested in people, not only in what they do, but who they are, in their intimate story, their twists and turns and pitfalls, their triumphs and disasters. All this leads to lessons to be learned, a deeper realization of life's wisdom unfolding.

When talking with people, give them the respect of listening with your entire being. People are very sensitive to you. If you are looking around, if you are ready to jump in the middle of what they are saying with ideas only you want to talk about, they notice.

Be careful not to interrupt when you add in an idea, as people really hate being interrupted whether they tell you or not. People want to be heard when they have something important to say. Make sure you hear it and let them express it.

This applies not only to business, but is even more vital with your family and children. Be absolutely attentive, not just pretending to be interested, not just acting as if what they are saying is worth listening to. Pay full attention and see if you can find the golden nuggets in what others are saying. See if you can read more into their ideas and thoughts from their body language, their intonations of voice, their inflections, and discover what they really want or are trying to say. See how deep you can really get and communicate.

By being fully engaged in others you will be considered one of the greatest conversationalists in the world.

Many years ago, Dale Carnegie wrote that he was in line at a Western Union, and he saw the attendant, who was very plain, in almost every respect, and he was hard-pressed to find something, anything that was interesting about the young man.

Finally, when it was Carnegie's turn to be waited on by this young man, Dale said, "You have the most amazing and wonderful head of red hair."

The boy beamed, got so excited and began talking about how everyone told him that, and went on and on. Dale Carnegie said hardly a single word. And as he left, the young man said it was such a pleasure to talk to Carnegie and that he thought Dale was such a great conversationalist.

Sure you want to be eloquent, but nothing can take the place of being sincerely and intensely focused on another's life, in their world. Listen with your heart. Network with your heart. This will attract to you the people, friendships and relationships that not only will make your life and networking effective, but also will make each day extremely meaningful and rich.

Find, discover and learn. This makes your networking all about learning and finding ways to help others. Every single one of us can be more aware, more compassionate and empathetic, and listen as if it was, and it may very well be, the most interesting conversation we ever have had. This is truly the best way to begin and continue your networking and to grow yourself so as to meet the incredible opportunities you will discover.

Networking is an opportunity. Everyone you meet can be an opportunity. You just need to be of higher awareness to realize **the Power of ONE Business Connection**.

Made in the USA
San Bernardino, CA
15 February 2015